Praise for

Mountain Brew

"The homebrew revival has spawned its first new literature, a book that taps brewhouse knowledge and experience."

—*New Hampshire Times (1975)*

"More like a beer party than a brewing session . . . *Mountain Brew* packs a variety of recipes for every palate and a potpourri of beer anecdotes. The information is all there."

—*The Advocate (1975)*

"A slim classic. . . . Even before celebrity craft brewers came along, the hills of Vermont held earnest homebrewers who tackled lagers and ales with vigor. The strangely enchanting little tome offers a glimpse into that world. . . . It might not be the definitive guide to homebrewing, but it's a sweet keepsake of another age."

—*Seven Days*

"Set aside your dog-eared copy of *The Complete Joy of Homebrewing.* Eight years earlier—and two before the legalization of homebrewing—a merry band of Vermont homebrewers published their recipes and anecdotes in a slim book call *Mountain Brew*. There's more than a touch of rebelliousness in the tone. The homebrewing instructions are a casual narrative, and the ingredients would make a BJCP judge blanch, but the book is a hoot for anyone who wants a glimpse of the cultural origins of this immensely popular hobby. These sound like great folks to have a beer with."

—All About Beer Magazine

Mountain
Brew

*Earth Ponds: The Country Pond Maker's Guide to
Building, Maintenance, and Restoration*

Earth Ponds A to Z: An Illustrated Encyclopedia

Landscaping Earth Ponds

The Book of Non-Electric Lighting

Mountain
Brew

A High-Spirited Guide to Country-Style Beer Making

40th Anniversary Edition

TIM MATSON & LEE ANNE DORR

THE COUNTRYMAN PRESS

A division of W. W. Norton & Company

Independent Publishers Since 1923

The Countryman Press
www.countrymanpress.com

A division of W. W. Norton & Company, Inc.
500 Fifth Avenue, New York, NY 10110
www.wwnorton.com

For information about special discounts for bulk purchases,
please contact W. W. Norton Special Sales at
specialsales@wwnorton.com or 800-233-4830.

All photographs are courtesy of the authors except where
otherwise noted.

Printed in the United States

Mountain Brew
978-1-58157-308-4 (pbk.)

10 9 8 7 6 5 4 3 2 1

For all the drunks who didn't make it home

CONTENTS

FOREWORD

All it takes is a spark, an idea that becomes more than the sum of its parts. When *Mountain Brew* debuted, it was a perfect specimen of Vermont's future attitude towards beer. Only Tim Matson and Lee Anne Dorr never knew it. Tim and Lee Anne wanted better beer than what they could buy. In a time where brewing equipment was scarce, home-brewing illegal, and proper ingredients difficult to find, they embraced the situation. They built what was needed, grew their ingredients, and brewed it. So great was the journey, they published their adventures and sold it out of their car to anyone that wanted to buy it. They were one of the sparks that reignited Vermont's brewing industry.

Looking at Vermont's history in brewing, one

thing in particular stands out: the loss of brewing knowledge. With Vermont entering a self-imposed prohibition on beer and spirits in 1853, we effectively suffocated a brewing heritage that was just starting to get off the ground. One single brewer carried on his trade in Burlington until the 1880s. When he too gave up, so began a long brewing void in Vermont. While Vermonters were crafty in circumventing the law, state and federal prohibition stopped the legal commercial production of beer in the state for nearly a century.

Along with this noble failure of an experiment, we lost the knowledge of brewing within the state. All that was left in the 1970s beer world were mainly the remnants of World War II—American adjunct lagers and more flavorful imported beers. Aside from Fritz Maytag's endeavors at Anchor Brewing on the West Coast, the American brewing scene was limited to fewer than 100 breweries in 1975, most producing American lagers. None of those were in Vermont. With no real handbook on how to brew beer available, Tim and Lee Anne took the first step toward rebuilding our collective knowledge. Charlie Papazian's monumental work, *Joy of Home Brewing*, would come out a decade later, blowing off the door to the world of homebrewing that *Mountain Brew* had cracked open.

Rarely does someone write a book with the mindset of starting a wider movement. *Mountain Brew* was written as a guide on how to brew beer with a "by any means necessary" attitude for people just like Tim and Lee Anne. The first modern homebrewing book written since the repeal of Prohibition, it was published at a time when it was still illegal to produce homebrewed beverages in America. While the world of brewing has moved forward and the recipes featured here may not be up to the palates of brewers today, this work gives the history of where we (re)started. To understand these roots and how we evolved in the world of brewing is to take a fascinating look at technology, attitude, and development. Looking back at the forty years since *Mountain Brew* was first published, Vermont has become arguably one of the top regions of brewing in the country and even the world. It is time to grab a chair, pour a beer, and learn about an important moment in beer history.

Adam Krakowski
Montpelier, VT
2015

PREFACE TO THE 40TH ANNIVERSARY EDITION

This being the 40th anniversary of the publication of a long-lost beer making book (one that many consider one of the founding documents of the home-brew and craft beer movement) and having been tasked with concocting a tasty introduction to said book, I invite readers and brew lovers to travel back with me to the dark ages of American beer—the 1970s. Even in those macro-brewing days, a select few of us were toiling away on our own bewitching ales and lagers, produced under the most adverse and twisted of circumstances. Once quaffed, those beers led to the recipes and literary meanderings of the very book you now hold, scan, view, or whatever now passes for reading.

To share in the shenanigans of this time warp firsthand and generate your own original tasting notes, I recommend you skip this "behind the scenes" commentary and go directly to the original book, which begins on page 51. There, the flavor profile of the Seventies bursts forth like a juicy Vermont IPA (even though there was no such thing back then). Then, you can return here to see how these untutored fermentations could have erupted in the mountain landscape that was "Once Upon a Time" Vermont. Or if you prefer, quaff this introduction first. Either way, read responsibly.

Once Upon a Time in a Nova Far Away

Vermont in the Seventies was a proving ground for the early homebrew and craft beer revival. Or rather, re-revival. After all, America had over 1,000 regional breweries during the nineteenth and early twentieth century. But a combination of Darwinian economics and the temperance-inspired Prohibition left the country with a small fraction of those breweries after the 21st Amendment.

The survivors of Prohibition were dominated by big conglomerates like Budweiser, Schlitz, and

Coors. These resurrected beers had been reformulated to cut production costs and dilute the taste to appeal to a broader market. As William Knoedelseder notes in his book *Bitter Brew,* drinkers of traditional beer (Europeans mostly) took a pretty harsh view of Budweiser, seeing it as part of the Americanization of the world. For example, *The Economist* even went so far as to call Bud a "glass of water wasted." The rationale for making bland beer is simple: If you can produce a product with general appeal, amenable to mass manufacture and predictable distribution across the country, you can make a lot of dough. Adding insult to injury, as the rollback of Prohibition opened the tap on industrial light lagers, it neglected to repeal the part of Prohibition that outlawed home brewing beer. (Household wine making was okay for some reason, unconnected to the beer industry.) With the exception of expensive imports and the rare local, the avenues to quality beer procurement were mostly blocked.

Well, not quite. To understand how it is that a small north country mountain state could become a future pioneer and producer of craft beers, let's travel back to the late 60s and early 70s. A wave of young folks were moving into Vermont. Some were avoiding the Vietnam War, some were trying to recover from it. Shell shock lingered after the assassinations of JFK, Martin Luther King, Bobby Kennedy, Malcolm X, and a whole lot of activists and rabble-rousers in the student and black power movements. As Jimmy Carter put it, there was a "malaise" upon the land. An apocalyptic feeling was in the air. The U.S. was done for, we all thought.

Yet despite these currents of despair, Vermont held out a promising vision. It had a tradition of progressive activism going back to the Civil War Underground Railroad, and more recently the *Living the Good Life* writings of Scott and Helen Nearing, Ray Mungo's *Total Loss Farm*, and others. Vermont was mountainous and cold, with cheap land and plenty of it. Hippies, back-to-the-landers, vets, survivalists, and Whole Earth Catalogers came in droves. Dozens of communes sprang up. (See Pam, page 97) According to one estimate there were 35,000 hippies in the state in 1970. That's one third of the 107,527 population between the ages of 19 and 34.

A lot of those hippie immigrants were thirsty. A number knew from their foreign travels, especially to English pubs, that good beer did exist. They knew there was an active homebrew culture in England, and an obscure beer making prohibition—especially one imposed by the "establishment"—would not deter these pioneers. Legality was not a big consideration for the new Vermonters.

I arrived in Vermont in 1971. I was a twenty-eight years old Army veteran. Drafted for a two year stint in 1966, I got lucky and avoided 'Nam. Instead, I wound up working on a newspaper at Fort Bragg, where I learned more about writing and journalism than I had in college English. In 1968, I got out and signed on as an editor at a publishing house in New York. Exciting times, but after three years and a few vacation trips to Vermont, my girlfriend and I quit our jobs and headed north in a red VW bug. We took out a mortgage on an old farm in Strafford. She worked for a Montessori school, and I applied myself to apprenticing the rural arts, beginning as a novice carpenter for $2.50 an hour. The skills to survive in the north were not taught in a class. It was live and learn. Construction. Gardening. Fish farming and pond building. Wood heat. Raise and slaughter livestock. And, of course, make beer.

. . .

January 1976. Girlfriend No. 1 is gone. So is the farm. I have moved to the other side of town, built a cabin on forty-five acres of mountain forest, and live without electricity or running water. I practice all my recently learned survival skills. I have a portable Tandberg short wave radio and listen to a lot of Bachman-Turner Overdrive. I have a Kimball upright to annoy the mice, but it's rarely in tune. Wood heat is murder on piano sounding boards.

And I have a new girlfriend. She lives a mile down the road. Depending on the weather and vehicle viability, we visit by foot or car, usually to make beer. We have become gung ho brewers.

Today we are going to hit the road with a trunkful of our own mountain brew. And *Mountain Brew*. Over the past summer Lee Anne and I have been collecting beer recipes from local brewers. We've put in some of our own recipes and concocted a few oddball stories to add to the mix. The result is a slim, thirty-two page volume that sells for $2.25. I am about to learn the skill of the hand sale.

Knowing just enough about publishing to be dangerous, I proposed the book idea at the end of a long night of bottle capping and spillage swilling. We were not the sort of purists who waited around for all capped bottles to mature. Spillage is fully fermented kin to English pub ale. Fresh, flat, and delicious.

On this chilly January morning, we load the books in Lee Anne's very faded blue Chevy Nova. There is some kind of a recession or depression going on as usual, which has little meaning up here. Up here it's always a depression. Wage work is scarce, and this book idea of mine arose out of necessity as much as passion for brewing. We love our beer and we need money to make it, so why not sell a how-to book to our fellow Vermonters?

In the trunk we have the precious books and, just as valuable, several bottles of homemade parsnip wine. We have learned in our travels that transporting beer to yonder potluck or barn raising is likely to end in geysers of foam if uncapped too soon. Or even explosions. Better to bring the wine.

As short as the January days are, it is good that we started at sunrise, because after less than thirty miles one of the wheels flies off. The car shudders violently, and as Lee Anne pulls over I see the tire rolling down the bank into the woods. By some quirk, the car remains upright like a tricycle. It takes hours to find the wheel, but we are relieved to discover that the tire has not been damaged. Lee Anne says that during a recent tire change the lug nuts must not have been tightened properly. Who was involved in the tire change I decide not to ask.

"It looked like a bottle cap blowing off," she says. She proposes we use the event in a future story, the existential meaning of which she will meditate on. We never will decode the message, and sadly Lee Anne won't live to see the 40th anniversary publication, but I mention it here because it is the sort of synchronistic mystery she always liked. Puzzles without answer. (See the last lines of "Flood of '76," on page 78, for reference.)

The trip north is our first road-selling adventure, and we stop in every town with a bookstore or health food shop. I have made several critical mistakes in this self-publishing project, and it is in the bookstores that I begin to discover my blunders. To the booksellers, the meaning of our book is as mysterious as the meaning of the rolling tire. The cover shows a pink mountain and a red sunset, with *Mountain Brew* in tiny letters near the bottom. The image is striking in its abstract simplicity, and is in fact derived from a painting by Lee Anne's nine-year-old daughter Heather. Beautiful artwork, all agree. The problem is the title. It is so small! However enticing it might be, it will be lost on most shelves with a rack at the bottom. And what, the storeowners ask, does it mean anyways? No authors' names, no clue as to category or subject. Is it fiction or fact? Poetry? Cookbook? Children's book? To twenty-first century eyes, the first edition cover looks pretty clueless. On the other hand, it is quite in tune with the pigeonhole resistant contents. In fact, it is a cookbook. It is poetry. It is fiction. It is non-fiction documentary. It's all of those things, but most of all it's homebrew.

Our potential bookseller isn't done puzzling yet. In our efforts to be frugal, we used a small font for the text and compressed the sections together. That cut costs on paper, but there weren't enough signatures to support a real binding. Therefore the book had to be stapled. Thus, when slipped into a shelf and flanked by other books, it becomes invisible. What had I been up to during those years in publishing? Had I learned nothing? I blame it on the three-hour expense account lunches.

Despite the flaws, we manage to sell a surprising number of books. The health food stores dig it the most. After all, the local health food shop is where homebrewers in the Seventies get their beer yeast and hops. (In a pinch, bread yeast and hopped malt extract do just fine.) True, homebrewing beer was still illegal, but health food stores did sell winemaking supplies (legal to do at home), and the wholesalers must have slipped some beer ingredients into the mix, because, well, canned malts from Britain lined most shelves. I never saw a treasury agent hiding behind a five gallon carboy. In fact, the health food stores carried all manner of brew equipment, from cappers as big as car jacks to brew pails and hydrometers. I guess if push came to shove, brewers could claim they were making wine. Yeast, sugar ... it's really all the same thing, eh? What a goofball law!

Anyway, our first sales trip was offering some valuable lessons about the book business. Here's another good one. When a book sells for $2.25 and you give a 50% discount to the store, you have a long way to go before you have a down payment on a replacement Nova. Nevertheless we sell several cartons of books all over the state, despite the nebulous cover. Something heady is in the air.

...

We didn't know it, but about the same time *Mountain Brew* hit the shelves, the first pamphlet-sized incarnation of Charlie Papazian's bestselling *The Joy of Home Brewing* was finding its way out of the Colorado Rockies. Michael Jackson's *World Guide to Beer* was published in 1977, and would go on to stimulate high regard for quality beers. Also in the 1970s, Fritz Maytag was turning a failing San Francisco brewery into the Anchor Steam Beer Company, which many consider the first microbrewery of the current craft beer generation.

Lee Anne and I got back from our bookselling adventure and life went on. We did some more brewing, started a community garden with a bunch of folks on the road, and sold another printing of *Mountain Brew* with the more informative cover—with a new subtitle, *A High Spirited Guide to Country-Style Beer Making*—and some nice reviews on the back. Gradually we drifted apart. Lee Anne had family obligations, and I had a house to finish building. But apart or together, we kept making beer.

With homestead improvements on the front burner, I wasn't thinking about the book until one

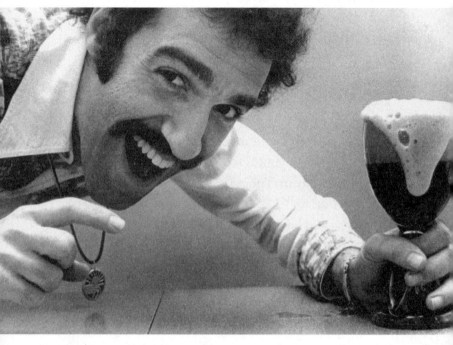

Charlie Papazian, author of The Joy of Home Brewing, *in 1977*
(Courtesy of Charlie Papazian)

summer day in '78 when an enterprising journalist showed up at my place with a dog-eared copy of *Mountain Brew* in hand. His name was Stephen Morris, and he told me he was a fan of the book, a devotee of homebrewing, and had just embarked on a cross country road trip (with his pregnant wife and pet dog) to chronicle the state of American regional breweries. He feared they were a dying species, and his trip would be a rolling wake for the beloved beers we were losing to the Bud and Coors bulldozers. Morris had spent a year in England, fallen in love with local pub beers and pub culture, and taken up homebrewing, which was popular there. Reading *Mountain Brew* he thought he saw the spark of a potential homebrew movement in the U.S. What did I think? A pleasant interview ensued, I wished him good luck, and he gathered his family in the van and asked for directions to the nearest hillbilly roadhouse.

Years later, a copy of *The Great Beer Trek* turned up in the mail. Morris had made his cross-country beer odyssey and found the regional breweries in a dire state. Here and there he found some hardcore hangers on, such as Yuengling and Straubs in Pennsylvania, and Matts and Genesee in New

York. I was flattered to be the lead off interview in the book (which you can read an excerpt of in the Afterword on page 115, but rescue hopes for American regional beers looked dim.

But something magical happened in the eight years it had taken Morris to get his book into print. Interest in regional brewing built up steam. By 1986, the Boston Beer Company had started brewing a regional beer called Sam Adams. Here in Vermont, the Catamount Brewery opened in White River Junction, and many contend it was the first microbrewery in the east. Up north in Burlington, Greg Noonan opened the Vermont Pub & Brewery in Burlington, one of the first brewpubs in the country.

How do you account for this spontaneous burst of regional brewing activity, after so many years of prohibition-induced drought? I credit it to homebrewing. Steve Mason, chief brewer and co-founder of Catamount, had been a homebrewer. Greg Noonan began as a homebrewer during his college years in New Hampshire. And Charlie Papazian's *The Joy of Home Brewing* was on its way to selling a million copies. He had been homebrewing since the '60s.

Mashing a batch (Courtesy of Charlie Papazian)

In addition to the influence of homebrew on the creation of what would become the phenomenon of craft beer, there was Vermont. You can't exaggerate the influence of Vermont on the growth of craft beer, nano beer, micro beer, artisanal beer, or whatever you like to call it. After Catamount came Otter Creek, Long Trail, Magic Hat, and dozens of others that continue to multiply today. It is said that per capita there is more craft beer in Vermont than any other state, and that more beer is produced here than in Eastern Europe. Three of the most esteemed breweries in America come out of Vermont: Hill Farmstead in Greensboro, Lawson's Finest Liquids in Warren, and The Alchemist in Waterbury, whose double IPA Heady Topper might be the most sought-after beer in the world. Buyers line up at dawn on designated sale days in a few Vermont outlets, and scalpers drive to New York to sell them for $20 a can.

Why does Vermont make such good beer? I've heard different explanations. It's the do-it-yourself ethic. It's locavore. Small is beautiful. Maybe it's the mountains, which separate the towns into independent fiefdoms, each cultivating its own unique brew. Maybe it's the water, whose blend of minerals and pH is especially friendly to ale fermentation. (Steve Mason is said to have chosen White River Junction for the site of Catamount, the state's first craft brewery in 1986, for the favorable water.) Maybe it's the cold climate, unfriendly to wine grapes, but always ready for a fire. After all, beer-making starts with a hot soup of malted grains.

Another possibility came to my attention in the book *Vermont Beer*, a fascinating history and brewery guide by Kurt Staudter and Adam Krakowski. Little mentioned in Vermont beer books or general state histories is the self-imposed alcohol prohibition here from 1856 to 1933, when national prohibition ended. Due to temperance movements and religious influences, the legislature made Vermont a dry state during this period. Thus, unlike many surrounding states, after the mid-nineteenth century Vermont had no legal breweries. (Ironically, around the same time we were the second biggest hop producer in the country.) As a result, there was no tradition of established breweries to restart after Prohibition. It took a wave of rebel back-to-the-landers to fix that.

A motley crew of homebrewers celebrating the Great American Beer Fest in 1986 (Courtesy of Steve Polewacyk)

Message in a Bottle

Reading *Mountain Brew* all these years later is like finding a message in a bottle. The message? It's the crazy Seventies and we're making beer and fightin' the power. Check out these recipes!

A lot of people think the hippie era was a waste of time. Peace, love, and understanding? Yeah, right. And in many ways it's true. How many wars since Vietnam? Not enough fingers and toes for that. But if our generation didn't pull off the Age of Aquarius, at least give us credit for starting the Age of Craft Beer. Not to mention that, a couple of years after *Mountain Brew* was published, homebrewing beer was legalized. I don't remember if it was before or after legalization that I sent a copy of the book to President Jimmy Carter, but I did. Later on, a letter arrived from the White House. It was a Thank You note signed by the President. Did he really have the time to read it? Maybe. But I'll bet his brother did. Billy Beer, anyone?

The recipes in *Mountain Brew* do not come with the American Homebrewers Association Seal of Approval, if there is such a thing. In fact I've heard the recipes described by some readers as amateurish, misguided, and even appalling. I think such criticism misses the point, because there are many homebrewers and people in the craft beer business who love the book. Sure, you don't show up at Logan Airport expecting to ride a Wright Brothers biplane. But if you have an interest in aviation you might want to take a look at how that aircraft got off the ground. The thrills, the spills! Same for beer lovers. *Mountain Brew* is a magical mystery tour of the early days of the brew revolution.

The Mountain Brewers of Orange County were our friends and neighbors. They were eager to share their stories and recipes, but many of them insisted on using a *nom de biere*. Some of these folks had jobs where provocative opinions could get you fired, like for advocating anarchy and selling homebrew and libeling million dollar beer companies. The best tales are often told by Anonymous.

However, after a span of forty years, I suspect the statue of limitations has expired on homebrewing violations and no harm can come from pulling back the curtain just a bit on our accomplished cast. We'll stay in character throughout the rest of the original book by preserving pseudonymity, but we can flesh out the backstories a bit here. Besides, there was never much camouflage, even when Lee Anne and I first wrote it. Mostly we omitted last names, and once, unintentionally, we misspelled the first. The big switcheroo was transforming Lee Anne into Sue of "Sue's Brew." The name "Sue" was chosen because we couldn't think of a drink that rhymed with Lee Anne. Lee Anne and I may also be related to Susie and Billy in "The Flood of '76," but as a work of apocalyptic fiction, going there requires postmodern narrative exegesis, which doesn't mix well with homebrew.

So what kind of people were the brewers? Two or three, including Lee Anne, came from the South. With rebellion and moonshine in their blood, they were born to be brewers. Another southerner, Sid, was a brilliant computer engineer, played a mean pump organ, and liked to cook stir-fry in a wok. He helped invent one of the world's first electronic synthesizers. Pam and her husband ran one of the first farm communes in Vermont, raised a bunch of kids, and, being one of the few African Americans, pioneered diversity in our town. Martha loved farming, and, as she later wrote me, "played farm wife" through much of her life. Her beer was perhaps the most inventive of all. She experimented with all manner of adjuncts, such as wormwood, chamomile, and buckwheat. She lived in a farmhouse without electricity and kept her kerosene lamp chimneys polished bright.

Peter and Ina also lived beyond the electric line, and he worked as a builder. Come to think of it most of us lived without electricity, because you could get good land pretty cheap off the main line. This was before solar panels, so there was a lot of kerosene and 12-volt lights. It was common practice to carry car batteries inside at night to run a few lights and a radio. Michael, another brewer off the grid, hailed from New York City and often played an acoustic guitar. Rounding out the cast, John was a legendary hippie.

Looking over some of these recipes I'm a bit shocked at the amount of sugar called for. On the other hand, as it's made clear, these brewers were pinching pennies, and sugar was cheaper than malt, if malt was even available. Remember, gas prices were on their way to doubling. Inflation and interest rates were hovering around 10%. Sugar? Pour it on.

Or maybe not. As Michael encouraged us (see page 92), skip the sugar and make your own malt. He was getting down to the kind of malting that most home brewers shortcut today. Brew shops now sell powdered malt, liquid malt extract, and malted barley grains ready for the wort. But a virtuous homebrewer would start with barley grains that need to be soaked, sprouted, and dried to reach the cooking stage. The only way to be more self-sufficient would be to grow the barley yourself.

Lee Anne and I also preferred to shortcut the purist route, so it was either sugar or, when we could afford to splurge, Blue Ribbon malt. Blue Ribbon was always in stock down at Dan and Whit's in Norwich ("If we don't have it, you don't need it"). It was supposedly sold for cooking, but if that was true, why the hop flavoring?

It was an open secret that Blue Ribbon was used for homebrewing, federal offense or not. And Blue Ribbon sold plenty, enough in fact the keep the Pasbt brewing company out of bankruptcy during Prohibition. When Prohibition struck, the folks at Pabst took the malt they usually used to make their Blue Ribbon lager, and canned it for sale to "bakers." And like Betty Crocker or Aunt Jemima, Blue Ribbon put a motherly cameo of one lovely "Lena" on the label to assure us of the product's wholesomeness.

If you knew your brewing history, Lena looked

Cans of malt extract sold for "baking" (Courtesy of Charlie Papazian)

like she was winking at the whole charade. She could have been a secret symbol of the brewing tradition. Before guys like Busch, Miller, Pabst, and Coors commandeered the brewing business to turn it into a cash cow, women had been the beer makers. Beer was made at home, and mother made it with her own special recipe. Thomas Jefferson is known to have been a homebrewer, but it was his wife Martha who stirred the wort.

At the time *Mountain Brew* appeared, the beer business (retail and homebrew supplies) was dominated by men. Check the beer books appearing at the time, and the people running breweries large and small were guys. Were we breaking ground when we featured four women as our mountain brewers, including one as coauthor? Perhaps. But maybe it was the tradition calling. It came about as naturally as yeast turns sugar to alcohol. The girls were pals and they were making beer. In fact, the book itself was designed and printed by a feminist collective, The New Victoria Printers, in Lebanon, New Hampshire. They were cool, and they did good work. Whatever happened back then was just in the air. Today, of course, there are scores of women in the beer business.

It's worth reminding readers that this book is more history than how-to, and as sure as I am that there are inspiring methods, philosophies, and ingredients here, you will not want to emulate these brews without double checking the best practice recipes at your local brew supply shop or online supplier. For example, in the realm of cleanliness, the Mountain Brewers cover the spectrum on sanitation. Michael uses boiling water, Sue likes baking soda, Martha uses a bit of bleach, Tom simply rinses his used bottles when it's time for bottling. And nobody is too proud to skip bottling completely and ladle the brew right out of the barrel. Today there are sanitizing solutions that make it possible to clean your bottles and other equipment without scorching your fingers or messing around with bleach, which can be poisonous. Considering the amount of Internet chatter about spoiled batches or the brewer's runs, don't blow off sanitation.

The crowning moment in brewing is, of course, bottling—because it's the last step before tasting and enjoying. This is the part you really don't want to screw up or you can wind up with flat beer or exploding bottles. The best way to ensure proper carbonation when bottling is to use a hydrometer to make sure your sugars are all fermented off. Don't overprime the bottles with the last bit of sugar and you'll be just fine. Some brewers add a scootch of sugar to each bottle before capping, some mix in enough for the whole batch and then fill and cap. But if you add too much sugar, or don't keep the batch evenly stirred, you can get in trouble.

I've never had a bottle actually explode, just flying caps and a sticky puddle. But a badly overprimed beer can become a glass shattering bottle bomb. I remember making a special batch of dark ale in the late 1980s to celebrate the birth of my first child. A bunch of bottles blew their caps, and there's still a stain on one of the loft beams where I put the beer after bottling. I opened all the bottles, released the pressure, and recapped before any of them exploded. Then we took the beer to the hospital and toasted the birth with mother, brewer, and nurses. It tasted great.

Beer Thirty

Some parting comments before closing: A few years ago I noticed the first craft beers showing up with flavor additives—pumpkin, chocolate, spruce

Lee Anne's daughter Heather bottling homebrew with her dad
(Courtesy of Michael St. John)

spirals, and more. Lots more in fact. They were new on the beer scene, but it reminded me that Lee Anne and I had long ago experimented with additives, everything from mint to steak bones. Martha added Postum and various herbs. Tom liked apples and citrus fruits. Naturally, hops were in most recipes, whether in the malt extract, bought separately, or grown or gathered wild, the way Peter and Ina describe harvesting theirs.

Another place we were ahead of the curve was the cheerful anti-beer boosterism of the mountain brewers who'd cut way back on drinking or quit altogther. You are not likely find many teetotalers in brew books. A marketing no-no. Yet as Pam says, "That was the end of homebrew . . . we were sober." In fact the epigraph we start the book with might as well have come from Bill Wilson, fellow Vermonter and founder of Alcoholics Anonymous.

Finally, I'd like to raise a glass to Lee Anne, Pam, and John who have passed on, and to other mountain brewers who strayed off my radar. I was in touch with Martha recently, and her good spirits were spritzy as ever. This new publication has also given me a chance to catch up with Lee Anne's daughter, Heather, whose cover artwork gave the original book so much of its Vermont character. And thanks to you dear reader, brewer, drinker, or abstainer for coming along on this trip down the old homebrew highway. Enjoy the ride.

Tim Matson
Strafford, VT
2015

TIM'S *MOUNTAIN BREW*
ANNIVERSARY ALE

I brewed this beer in the winter of 2015 to celebrate the forty years since the first run of *Mountain Brew*. It's a light mild ale made with a mix of dried and liquid malt extract. This is a one-gallon recipe, which is an amount I like to brew because it's less hassle than the usual five-gallon recipes. No big boiling pots on the stove, and less heavy lifting and bottling chores. It also gives me a more opportunities to experiment with different beer styles: various types of malt, hops, yeast, etc. You can blow a batch, or simply not like it, without wasting a larger investment in time and ingredients.

Considering the amount of great beers available today, you have to wonder why people still brew at

Tim bottling a batch in the old days

all! I think it's the good old do-it-yourself life force fighting for air. When I moved to Vermont and started brewing, it wasn't just beer that folks were making. It looked like every other new house was owner-built. People worked on their cars, supplied their heat and lighting, and farmed a lot of food. So many of those options are gone now—lost to building codes, computerized vehicles, and less free time. But making beer lets you reclaim the creative process. I also like using my own spring water. I think it makes for better beer than even high-end craft brews, perhaps because it doesn't contain fluoride, chlorine, or any of those nasty chemicals. Best of all, I love to inhale the sweet atmosphere of bubbling malt and hops that fills the house at brewing time.

To get started, you'll need some basic brewing equipment. I have a three-gallon stainless steel pot for cooking the wort. You'll also need a long stainless steel spoon, a ladle, several measuring cups, some plastic tubing for siphoning, a primary fermenter with an airtight lid with an exhaust port, an airlock, a capper, and some bottles.

It helps to have a separate pot to decant the fermented beer into at bottling time. Everything should be super clean, from brewing equipment to bottles. Some folks use sanitizing fluid you can get at the brew shop. I use hot soap and water, then rinse everything well.

INGREDIENTS

1/2 pound dried malt extract
1/2 pound liquid malt extract
1 package ale yeast
1 oz. hop pellets (preferably Cascade or Brewer's Gold)
Sugar for bottling (I use table sugar, 10–12 tablespoons for the batch)

INSTRUCTIONS

Heat up a half-gallon of water. Add half of both types of the malt extract and lightly boil for 60 minutes, being careful to stir and not let the wort boil over. Add the remaining malts for last five minutes of boiling. Make sure to stir enough to keep the malts from caramelizing on the bottom of the pot.

During the boil, add 1/3 oz hops for the entire 60 minutes, 1/3 oz. hops for the last 30 minutes and 1/3 oz. hops for the last 5 minutes.

Turn off heat and add water to make one gallon. Stir and use hydrometer to test liquid for the potential alcohol content. It should read about 5 to 6 percent potential. (Some people use the brix scale, but the choice is yours.)

When liquid has cooled to room temperature, sprinkle the yeast on top and seal lid tight. Some brewers say you don't have to stir in the yeast, but I do. Insert airlock filled with water in port. The brew should start bubbling within 24 to 72 hours. Allow it to ferment for one to two weeks. After primary fermentation ends (the bubbling stops), check with a hydrometer. It should read close to zero on the alcohol scale, which means you've fermented off all the sugars.

Now siphon or pour off the brew into a clean container. Most brewers are careful not to stir up the lees before decanting, and you can use a strainer to keep out the dregs.

Next, add bottling sugar. I use regular table sugar, stirred into solution and then added to the container. You can also use dextrose, corn sugar, or other sweeteners. The question of how much sugar and what type for priming is hotly debated on the Internet. Every brewer seems to have different suggestions. It is true that once you've gotten this far, it's tragically possible to blow the whole batch (literally) by overpriming, or getting flat bottles by being too timid with the priming sugar. If you're unsure, try asking at your local brew supply shop or research online.

Once you have your brew ready to bottle, set the brew container at a higher level than the bottles. I usually put the brew on the kitchen counter, and the bottles on a short stool lower down. I put the bottles in a pot as I fill, to catch spills. Now siphon the brew into your bottles. Leave an inch or so of headroom in the bottles, and you're ready to cap. Let them sit for one to two weeks, then enjoy a cool, refreshing mountain brew.

Front cover of the original edition (1975)

"Caps ain't cheap anymore . . ."

This is about Beer

Not store bought. Homebrew. Homebrew is alive, like yogurt but without the strawberries. It's full of vitamins and minerals. And lots of carbohydrates too! And it gives you something to do. Same for those bottles filling up the yard. And that small budget. Or those food stamps that won't buy Pabst. You can bring in a good brew for a quarter a quart. Less if you concoct your own ingredients. For instance, make malt, grow hops, keep a strain of yeast, and pour in homemade maple syrup. Or drink it right out of the barrel, draft style. Saves time and caps.

Face it: Just about all American beer is bland and over-carbonated. The factories figured out that it's a lot cheaper to sell carbon dioxide than beer. With lots of interesting chemicals too. Not to mention inflated prices. Or the privilege of shuffling bottles around in advanced territories like Vermont and Oregon. It's enough to dry out the soggiest hillbilly. If you don't drink, it's enough to get you started. Either way you're cornered.

Homebrew is a way out. Homebrew is a different story. There really is no choice. Not after you've tasted a good brewer's best beer. So this is all about that—getting to know a good beer when you brew one. You can learn how to brew an excellent, reliable ale or lager. Just about the color of sunset. And cheap, with supplies from the local grocer. No fancy imports. Two pints and you're blissed. And if by chance you overload, relax. Homebrew hangovers are organic.

Questionables

*hat is swill?*
Store bought.

Which has more alcohol, homebrew or swill?
Homebrew.

Who invented homebrew?
Homer.

Who invented Homer?
Homebrew.

Can you bottle homebrew in bottles with twist-off caps?
You can, but why not use bottles that need a church
key instead? The glass is thicker and less likely to
explode.

Greg Noonan (top) and Steve Polewacyk (below) of the Vermont Pub & Brewery in Burlington, VT (Courtesy of Steve Polewacyk; photo by Jerome Noonan)

In Oregon and Vermont you pay five cents on the bottle when you buy beer. Are these bottles reusable? How come?

The reason you pay five cents on the bottle in Vermont and Oregon is that they don't want bottles on their highways. Instead, they grind them up and put them in the highways.

Did Tom Paine drink homebrew?

Yes, and after a lifetime crusading for revolution he died denounced as a drunk. After a comfortable period of decay, he was elevated to an American patriot.

Did our forefathers fight for the right to make homebrew in the Whiskey Rebellion?

Yes—and they lost. The winner was George Washington. His government proposed an excise tax on hillbilly brew, less for the revenue than to provoke resistance and bring clout to the states for the first time.

Was homebrew prohibited during Prohibition?

Yes, Prohibition prohibited it.

Do organic gardeners ever use homebrew in their gardens?

Yes. Slugs smell the homebrew fermenting in the little saucers and they come to drown. People can drown in it too.

How much does it cost to make free beer?
It costs about eight bucks to make ten gallons. That's less than twenty-five cents a quart. Trade half a batch at fifty cents a quart, and you have free beer!

Is it true that when you reach nirvana you sleep with your mouth open?
When did you arrive?

How come there's no ingredients label on beer bottles?
Nobody wants to know what chemicals are in beer. Because beer makes you forget what chemicals are in everything else.

How much homebrew can you drink before you've had enough?
Enough.

What is enough?
Enough is enough.

Sue's Brew

It's easy to make beer, and you almost can't go wrong. But there's a couple of things you have to be pretty diligent about, like cleanliness and watching the pot so it doesn't boil over. It is not true that a watched pot never boils. My brew has boiled over twice, and it's really messy.

You need tools and hard straight things—like thermometers and hydrometers—to make beer. And some fire, a four-gallon pot, a can opener that works, a big wooden spoon, two truly clean fifteen or twenty-gallon barrels, a funnel, a siphon tube, a pitcher, a box of caps, and a capper. You can usually get them at your friendly neighborhood grocery if you have five minutes for looking around.

Lee Anne (a.k.a. "Sue")

Also: a little beer yeast, a Sunday afternoon and some lovely Lena, that lady with the next-door face. She lives on the grocery store shelf in a can called Blue Ribbon Malt. Both Light and Pale Dry are good and are flavored with hops.

I think it's more fun to make beer with someone around, so I always go hunt down my neighbor who brews with me. We make ten gallons, drive each other crazy, and split it up after it's bottled. There is usually a batch brewing in the house. The guy down the road cleaned my distributor cap for a couple of quarts, and I trade homebrew for goat's milk. I still have to buy gas for my car, though.

Lovely Lena wants to stay in the can, so after you've gotten most of her out pour hot water in the can, stir, and then worry about something else for a while. Mix the two cans of malt with a gallon of water and put it on the stove in the four gallon pot. Put in eight pounds of sugar, stir, and don't go anywhere. This stuff on the stove is called wort. (Don't forget to spoon out the malt cans.)

Sugar is the cheapest sweetener, but molasses has a good flavor. Throw in a couple of cups of raisins too. Once I found some wild mint growing in the yard. I tied it up and put it in the pot while the wort was coming to a boil. Definitely left its flavor behind. An old timer told me to throw in a steak bone when everything was ready and brewing. I did. It was great beer. Lately, I've been hearing tales of chicken heads. You never can tell.

When it all starts to boil, stir and simmer for an hour. Somebody has to watch the boiling pot. Measure out nine gallons of water (for a ten-gallon batch you've already put in a gallon with the malt). The twenty-gallon barrel I use is a green plastic garbage can that I bought in the plastic store. They don't sell wood there anymore. Besides, plastic is cheap and it doesn't like bacteria. I always wash it out really good with hot water and baking soda after I'm done using it and before I use it again.

Now pour the wort in with the nine gallons of water. Then the yeast. Don't pitch your yeast into a hot brew. Fifty to seventy degrees is the right temperature. Two packages of beer yeast mixed with a cup of lukewarm water and a tablespoon of sugar is ready in thirty minutes. Squeeze in half a lemon. The last thing to add is a teaspoon of salt. Stir everything in the barrel around and put on the cover. Look the next day to see if it's fermenting. You can tell by the foam and bubbles on top.

Leave it alone for a few days and then check it with the hydrometer. Don't let the bugs in. It shouldn't take longer than two weeks. In the summer mine is ready in a week.

Hydrometers cost around five dollars. I've never made a batch without one, but some folks do. A hydrometer is made out of glass and it has numbers and lines on it. Try to get the kind with the red line at the top. When the hydrometer reads between the right lines, the message is clear: Bottle the beer.

When the beer is ready to bottle, plan on hanging around the kitchen for a while. Turn on the radio. Recruit anyone who can wash out a bottle. Friends are good for this. Put some baking soda in the sink with hot water and start washing. I really dig not using a bottlebrush because I'd rather shake than scrub. Get in the habit of rinsing out your home-brew bottles when you're done drinking. It's easier that way. I fill them up with soda water, put my finger in the top and shake hard and then let the water out. Then I run the tap water until the bottle is half full or so, shake again, pour everything out, and give it the eyeball scrutiny test. A lot of people use Clorox, and I would too if I didn't use soda. When the water gets sloppy, change it.

Meanwhile the finishing touches are ready for the homebrew. Lift the barrel up onto the table. Be gentle. That stuff on the bottom needs to stay on the bottom. Put in the siphon tube and start siphoning into the second barrel, which is sitting on the floor. It has to be a long hose, around four feet, and the bigger the hose the faster it goes. I tie a rock or clip a clothespin to the end so it won't flap around. The point is to get the homebrew from one barrel to the other, leaving the last three or four inches of dregs. You don't want that in your beer. Stir up the dregs and bottle two quarts. Throw the rest in the compost. Keep the quarts in a cool place and you won't have to buy yeast for your next batch. Don't reuse the yeast more than a couple of times before opening a fresh package.

What you have in the barrel is ready to be bottled. All it needs is a little zip because all the fizz is gone. It's turned to alcohol. The books say add two ounces of sugar per gallon of beer that is to be bottled. There's around eight gallons in the barrel—if you subtract the two quarts of draft beer you took off for the afternoon, the two quarts of yeast, and what you threw out. At eight gallons, that would be sixteen ounces of sugar, or two cups. I put in one and a half because that's just the way I am.

I've had a bottle of homebrew explode on me, and it's like a bomb. It happens when there's too much sugar in the bottle and it doesn't have anywhere to go. So don't screw up. Mix the sugar with four cups of water and heat on the stove until the sugar is dissolved. Stir into the barrel of siphoned beer at the point of bottling. Several times during the bottling, stir the brew because the sugar has a tendency to settle.

Take the four-gallon pot, fill it full of bottles, and start pouring. A funnel is really nice. Naturally it should be clean, like the pitcher and like your hands. You should be having a process going on. Someone at the sink washing bottles, someone pouring, and someone capping. Don't let the filled bottles hang around too long without caps. Five or ten minutes at the most. I got my bottle capper at a rummage sale for a dime. I didn't make homebrew at the time, but it had an interesting shape.

Put the finished product in the cellar or in the closet. Leave it alone for two weeks.

Now follow this recipe for these different brews. We've tried them all.

Each batch is different. My favorite for tight times is Flood of '76 Lager.

FLOOD OF '76 LAGER

2 cans Blue Ribbon malt extract, preferably Light
8 lbs. sugar
1 1/2 cups honey (optional)
2 cups raisins (optional)
2 packages lager yeast or home bottled yeast (use
    bread yeast in an emergency)
1 teaspoon salt
1/2 lemon squeezed
10 gallons water

FADE-OUT LAGER

3 cans malt extract

5 lbs. honey

2 bottles dark corn syrup

1/2 lemon

1 1/2 teaspoons salt

2 packages lager yeast

10 gallons water

ROLLER COASTER FLOAT

2 cans malt extract

12 cups sugar

2 cups maple syrup

2 cups light corn syrup

2 cups dark molasses

2 packages ale yeast

1 lemon

1 1/2 teaspoons salt

10 gallons water

BARBAROUS PORTER

3 cans malt extract
3 bottles dark molasses (24 ounces each)
6 lbs. sugar
1 lemon
3 packages ale yeast
1 tablespoon salt
14 gallons water

BONE BEER

2 cans malt extract
5 lbs. sugar
2 lbs. brown sugar
l lb. light corn syrup
1 lemon
1 1/2 teaspoons salt
2 packages ale yeast
1 steak bone
10 gallons water

The Flood of '76

It had been a very bad year and Susie had gotten into too much trouble. She tried to quit smoking twenty-two times. Twenty-two different brands. Finally, she switched to smoking mint.

It started to rain. It rained for a long time. It started to snow. It snowed for a long time. It started to blow. It blew the house away. Susie's mud puddles didn't grow. Her luck ran out.

She started down the road. There weren't any cars. Rich people are losing their brains, she thought to herself. She twirled her umbrella in an absent-minded way. Her mind was absent.

On the other side of the mountain things weren't much better. The flood had come. There was nothing to do. Susan met her neighbor on the road. He was wearing boots and he littered his bottles on the side of the road for the first time. Rich people are losing their houses, he thought.

"Wish we had some whiskey," she hollered out.

"It's a beautiful day," he said.

"I lost my house in the deluge," she said. "It floated away." Her mind had floated away too.

"We've got to do it today," he said.

"Do what?" she said.

"Make some beer. This is my last bottle," he said, tossing it 'til it spun in the air.

"If you didn't drink beer you'd never run out," she said.

Boredom decreases in reverse proportion to the rising of the flood. Except in town. In town, the flood is on television. In town, there's lots of money for swill. It's different in the hills. Floods, for instance. They really happen. There's no choice. They won't switch off.

"Let's brew something up," he said. He had a mind of his own.

"I think we should," she said. "But if the grocery

store is in town and the town didn't get washed away, how come there's Blue Ribbon malt floating down the road?"

He looked puzzled. "There's so much in life that is unexplainable," he said.

"How do you explain it?" She stopped and stooped over and gathered up some of the cans floating by. And that was the beginning of flood of '76 lager.

Technology is going down so fast you can't keep up with it. Or maybe it's the humidity. The greenhouse effect. Anything grows in a greenhouse. Except rocks. People try hard not to care about the rocks. But it's hard. The truth is though that beer comes from rocks. Since rocks were there first, before the Indians. What do we do with rocks? Gouge them out and run highways through them. Those rocks never grow any corn or hops. And corn and hops make beer.

The house was home away from home. Hardly any damage had been done. It sat by the road. She couldn't have dreamed it up if she tried. She tried to remember where her house had been. It's more

Not-my-own cellar

beautiful than before, she thought. I wonder if it still has carpenter ants?

"We'll have to go get your mailbox," he said.

She said, "When people don't read their mail, Billy, they don't want their bills."

"I'd like to bubble like I bubbled when I drank home brew," he said.

"Let's brew it again," she said. "Like it used to be."

They walked in. It was just like it used to be. There was nothing to do. They put the Blue Ribbon on the table.

"You can't make beer with just Blue Ribbon," he said. "Our only chance is down in the cellar."

The cellar was there, just like it used to be for somebody else. "It's weird," she said, "going down into not-my-own cellar."

She's weird, Billy thought.

They were looking for yeast. They found it in the old wooden barrel that Grandpa used. His diary was in there too. Billy had paid too much money for the windmills that powered his flashlight. The thought of it made him sick. But he could read the lines and he even read between the lines:

"A chipmunk couldn't live on five acres," Grandpa began. "But if they'd pull their own weeds and leave my weed alone, I could. I'm down in the cellar to find out what is under mind. Good things happen underground. Brews brew, carrots grow, and corpses rot. Wines grow old and excellent in the cellar. There's something steady about the cellar. It holds everything up and it just stays cool."

Susie and her neighbor's feet were getting wet. Susie looked around and said, "Shit a goddamn—the furnace is still going! Pull up a stump." Billy sloshed over and sat down by the warm stove. He read Grandpa's magic out loud:

Things are different up on top. Sometimes when the cloudy gray sky looks like a brain, it will rain, the way it's raining today. You can get hit by lightning up on top. But after 76 years I'm smoothing out and I haven't got hit yet. I think there's a flood coming and it may wash me away. It's been coming down for a long time and now it is starting to pour.

Billy read to Susie because Susie couldn't read. She'd lost her place. His eyes turned red. "You'd be surprised what your eyes do to see through the dark," he said.

"Why does it always pour?" she asked.

"So the rocks can turn into dirt," he said.

"Most of the people I know have rocks for brains," she said. "It's coming down hard and they're up to their ears."

But you can dwell in the cellar for only so long before you get thirsty. Susie and Billy are ready to brew. They'll trade five pounds of time for five pounds of sugar anytime. But they won't trade five pounds of time for five pounds of money. Human nature hasn't changed a bit. There's always somebody who won't sell out.

Susie was loaded. So was her gun. There was only one way to open the cans of malt: shoot off the tops. The can opener was gone, and so were some of the dogs.

"It's always going to be a struggle," he said. "As long as we choose to do this kind of thing. We only have eight pounds of sugar. That's not enough. Where's the honey, honey?" She said, "What do you mean honey? Where's the money, honey?"

She thought, thank god for the roots. They don't

mind the rain. They follow the rules that come down in the rain. It used to be chickens and roosters before it was chickens and eggs. Now it's chicken and noodles and it's getting to be chicken and stars. I can't find the honey. Only the stars.

The homebrew was bubbling. It made friends with the air. It smelled like a riddle. It puzzled them both. How can you talk about love when you don't mean what you say. How can you say what you mean when you don't mean what you say? It's just words going up into smoke like the head on a beer. You don't drink the head and you can't eat the words.

Mountain Brewers
ORANGE COUNTY, VERMONT

Martha

I like to keep away from fancy equipment and ingredients and make it more like down home concocting. Pinch-and-dash style cooking. Mad chemistry. In other words, not too much by the books. Therefore, I've almost always used Blue Ribbon malt. I like to replace or add to the hops with yarrow or wormwood. Wormwood is in the family of absinthe, which some say has a narcotic effect. I think one of these bitter, sedative herbs is a must. Use the whole plant, even the root. I also like to add mint, chamomile, clover, coltsfoot, comfrey, or other healthful herbs. You can barely taste them but it makes me feel like I'm sneaking a health

Wormwood (Courtesy of H. Zell)

elixir in the guise of booze. Sometimes I put in some Postum for dark malt. I always get so blissed on brew I can never analyze the various effects. Or maybe it's more that I don't care to—it takes away from the pleasure of the moment or something.

I had a friend who put in lots of Maxim to make a speedy beer. I thought it was awful but it got all drunk up (natch). I put in 17 teaspoons of salt to prime one batch before I noticed that the bag in my hand wasn't sugar. I went ahead and bottled it hoping aging would help. It didn't, though I had a friend lush enough to consume it. Another friend got sick of his beer getting drunk green so he made it with lots of garlic. It was terrible green, but after a year he said you couldn't taste the garlic and it was great. Another friend puts in lots of citrus (a dozen oranges per ten gallons). Many people like this and it produces a nice light color. Too much like carbonated grapefruit juice for me, though. But then I prefer a deep dark beer. Guinness Stout is my all-time favorite beverage (besides spring water).

Good water makes a difference in brewing, of course. I also added good flavor one time with burdock root. Chopped small, and boiled and strained off. Also, boil buckwheat groats and use the water.

These two give a good earthy flavor. Certainly healthful.

The first time I brewed was about twelve years ago. We bought the spiffy stuff from a brew supply store. Corn sugar and powdered malt. Our recipe said it should be bottled when it had a lacy pattern of bubbles on the top. I'd grab a bus home on lunch hour every day towards the end to make sure the lacy pattern wasn't gone. We were so afraid it would be flat. We had forty quarts under the bed and were rudely awakened one night by wet explosions. We lost most of it. I didn't brew again until three years ago. Since then I've stuck to it.

MARTHA'S RECIPE

6 lbs. malt extract and 5 lbs. sugar (dark)

or

3 lbs. malt extract and 10 lbs. sugar (light)*

2 to 3 ounces hops or other bitter herb

2 to 3 tablespoons salt (brings out flavor)

1 package ale yeast

Options:

1 or 2 oranges or lemons including juice and
    grated rind

1/4 cup ginger (fresh grated is best)

Grains or roots of your choice to steep in the water
    beforehand

In 4 or 5 gallons of H_2O, dissolve the sugar and the
malt and boil for 20 minutes.

* Or, to be outrageous, 6 lbs. malt, 10 lbs. sugar, and two
packages of yeast

Fresh hops ready to be picked (Courtesy of Kris Anderson)

Separately steep hops (don't boil). Pour these in a crock and add cold water.

Dissolve the yeast in warm water with some sugar, and add to the brew when it's lukewarm. Add the ginger and oranges. The citrus helps with the action, and the ginger is for flavor and a nose-tickling fizz effect.

Stir, cover, and keep in a warm place. I cover with a piece of plastic with elastic around it. Every time I pass by I sneak it open enough for my nose and breathe deeply and hold on tight. That intoxicating happy high is my favorite part of the whole thing. Watch out you don't keel over though. The first day or so will produce lots of foam scum, which I skim off as it rises.

As for where to incubate it, I always live with wood heat and put the brew near the parlor stove in winter and upstairs where the heat rises in summer. Let it work until bubbles stop coming. Prime the crock with one teaspoon sugar per pint (1 1/2 cups for ten gallons) before bottling.

For bottling I prefer quarts and pints. I wash them in a weak solution of Clorox and rinse well. Put as many bottles as fit in a big washtub and catch the spills as you bottle. Then cap 'em. Put them in a warm place for a few days and then move them into a cool place for two months (ho ho). Open a bottle after the first couple of days to make sure you didn't bottle too soon. If it fizzes over in the first three days, better uncap them SLOWLY and let them fizz out and recap. It's a drag, but it's better than exploding bottles.

MARTHA'S RECIPE

Sid

A lot of people get off on how rotten a home-brew they can drink. They get some kind of macho number off of drinking really foul alcohol. But have you tried any Budweiser lately? I mean, Budweiser is really bad. It doesn't taste good. And it's got almost no alcohol in it. Where I come from in West Virginia, the beer is 3.2% alcohol. That's it. You drink and drink and drink and nothing happens. Except you feel worse and worse. So as a result, everybody drinks hard liquor down there. You very quickly learn there's no point in hacking away at the beer bottles, so it's off to the state liquor store for a fifth of this or a fifth of that—but then that's a whole 'nother story.

There are really a lot of reprehensible dudes out there that are ready to sell poison for alcohol if the atmosphere is right. At some brewery out in the Midwest, some guy found out that if you put cobalt—just trace of cobalt—in a batch of beer it made, like, a super head. A really good head that just stayed there even after you'd poured the glass. Overnight even. Now whether you think that's groovy or not, well, they apparently thought it was alright, so they started a big ad campaign about how they had a really neat head on their beer. A year or so later, people started developing weird maladies that were eventually traced to ingestion of cobalt. So they quit putting cobalt into beer. It all probably has something to do with the laws of thermodynamics. The first law says that you can't win. The second law says you can't even break even.

It's illegal to sell homebrew. You're not supposed to. So you and I can't just go out and set up stills or whatever and make something groovy. Things are illegal because there's a lot of money to be made. It's sort of like it takes one to know one, right? And they know that there are certain forms of undesirable activity having to do with alcohol or what have you. The only thing is that there's a duality working there, which says that when it becomes illegal you encourage the most undesirable elements to keep doing it. For a lot of reasons. Laws like that are really stupid. Hopefully we can eventually evolve beyond a need for any laws at all.

Back when the sugar was so expensive, I tried brewing a bran beer. It's a cheap economy brew. I was trying to use the bran as a sugar substitute, something for the yeast to work on. I tried following a recipe for bran ale I'd found in a book. The problem with the bran, though, is that if you just dump it in, it makes a lot of sediment that you can never get rid of. The sediment doesn't solidify and form a nice cake down at the bottom of the bottle. And you can't strain it. You try cheesecloth or what have you—anything, really—and it either clogs the strainer or it goes right through. You have so many inches of solids afterwards, which are, regardless of what they say in the book, relatively undrinkable. Not pleasurable certainly. And that's wasted material. The more solids you have in suspension, the more comes through.

When you're fermenting, there's a lot of activity in the tub, and it keeps getting stirred up. When the yeast starts to die and the sediments fall down to the bottom, ideally everything would fall out and you'd make a cake. That's why some people use finings, which is just gypsum that settles down through there and pushes it literally to the bottom so the sediments don't come up when you bottle. So I buy the line that you should start out with as few solids as possible. The problem with the bran was that it's got particles of all sizes. While it's good and it smells good (like breakfast food) and it's cheap, it just doesn't seem to be one of your preferred beers. It tasted good, but it was just too murky.

The other thing is that when you have a solid in suspension it gives you a phony hydrometer reading. The hydrometer reading should be of dissolved sugar, like sugar and water. Sugar dissolves in water, and that's what the hydrometer is calibrated for. I mean, hell, that's the only thing that's going to make alcohol! The solids suspended in there ain't going to make alcohol. The object of the game is to make alcohol, isn't it?

Now theoretically you can convert the bran to sugar. But you've got to have a diastatic enzyme that converts starch to sugar. Keep the thing at 150 degrees for a couple of days and you can make all the sugar you want for peanuts. Actually, you could probably make it *from* peanuts, too. But peanuts probably cost more than sugar anyway. Now that sugar prices are down there's no big sweat. So go out and buy some sugar.

I'm a believer in ale yeast; I think that's where it's at. My bran beer was from a lager yeast, but it should have been from an ale yeast. Hard water, ale yeast. Soft water, lager yeast. Where I used to live in Vermont, the water was contaminated by copper and the homebrew was bad. I got hold of a book published by Guinness on industrial biochemistry, which mostly had to do with the manufacture of alcohol, saying that any kind of metallic ion is very bad news for beer yeast. Or industrial yeast, period.

This still leaves the problem of how you get over the taste of that canned malt, which I think has a taste that will take over anything.

Michael

I guess I didn't drink beer until I came up to Vermont. I wasn't much of a drinker. My friend Cathy was making beer. I was impressed. I walked right into it. With only food stamps, I could make big batches of beer. For very little money. That's the best way. The government gives you that money and lets you buy sugar and malt. Then you've got beer. You can get stoned for very little money.

So here I am now making my own malt. You just gotta sit down and make some malt, mister! That's really where it's at. It's so cheap. You go out and spend about ten bucks for a fifteen gallon batch. Well, I can make that same amount of beer for about four dollars. Because the malt is really cheap when you make it yourself. Buy some whole corn, or grow it, and take it from there. Far as I'm concerned that's really where it's at. Deaf Smith whole yellow corn. Sprout it, roast it, soak it overnight and then cook it. That's malt! I sprout it in a big way, starting with a four gallon container and filling it half full with corn. Sprout it right up. It gives me my choice of what I want. I can make dark, medium, or pale dry. And I can make bread with it. Actually, I find myself using malt more in pastry than in anything else, making rye bread and whatnot. I store the malt easily. After roasting I just take it out and wait to crack it when I'm ready. It works. That's how they're all making beer in the factories. Same way.

The night before brewing I soak the malt. I take a good mix of dark, medium, and light and coarse crack it. Put that in an enamel pail and soak it overnight. A big change happens overnight. The diastase starts to work and the water changes color. It becomes something obviously different. And then you go on from there and do your mashing up to 145 degrees or so. Steeping it overnight is really an important thing, because otherwise you stand over it all day, right? Waiting for the stuff to warm and it doesn't do very good. Much more hip to soak it overnight.

I want to start sprouting some rice. And malting rice. Brown rice. The Chinese do it. Americans and Europeans never do it. Oh, Budweiser has a little rice. But the Europeans never do it as far as I know. The Japanese and Chinese are also into a different kind of fermentation. They're into enzyme fermentation. It's a whole 'nother ball game. Sake is enzyme fermentation as opposed to yeast. It's pepsin. You take a little malt and chew it and spit it into the wort. You've heard of a steak bone or a cock's head thrown into the brew? That's your enzyme trip. It's fermentation, it's all fermentation.

For cleanliness I'm into Clorox. It will stop vinegar, strep, a lot of things. Hops are important also. Hops will prevent vinegar every time. Put the hops right to it and you won't ever get a batch of vinegar. Don't be fooled by Blue Ribbon. You don't really have many hops in there. Not much, comparatively minute. But hops are so expensive now. God, they jumped in price so much. Hops are worth a lot of money, mister! If you can find some that are growing somewhere, well, good for you. Otherwise cultivate them.

For bottling I give a good rinse in cold water after I'm finished drinking. And then when it's time to bottle, I rinse them in cold water and plenty of Clorox. I dip them into the pail, give them a shake and pour out. Then I go after them with boiling water. And it sterilizes. I mean, I'm not worried about my bottles. I boil water on the stove and I take it boiling in the kettle and pour into each bottle and scorch my fingers. For bottles I like the pint best. It makes a mellower beer every time. Of course, every bottle is different. A quart might be green when a pint's ready. You have to leave at least an inch of air when you cap the bottle. Keep in mind your prime, the sugar at bottling. I actually underprime because I'm going to fill them up a little fuller. A bottle that doesn't get filled enough gets too hot, too spritzy. There is too much air, too much room. You got to have some air, but not too much. Better flat than too spritzy.

There aren't many commercial beers I'm interested in, domestic especially. But Narragansett Porter—there's a different one. I'd like to see how they make that one. They're doing something special. I can't touch it. You can't make it with any of the ingredients around here. But most American beer is just a myth. Coors is just like Budweiser. Just a damn myth. Their big trip is that they are into everything—canning, trucking, brewing, everything. But far as I'm concerned, Coors is pretty poor beer. Got no zip; can't taste the hops. Give me Budweiser over Coors any day. Or Black Label or Genesee. They're all the same anyway. They all taste the same. Coors, ugh! At best, it's just a right wing organization.

You know what makes homebrew so good? American beer is so bad. They want to distribute it so widely they won't allow any local brewing. Local brewing is discouraged. All these beers like Schaefer and Budweiser used to be local breweries back in the days when you were allowed. Now you aren't allowed. Too many regulations, restrictions ... I don't know how it happened. And homebrewing is illegal. Far as I'm concerned I've got a right to make it. And sell it too.

Pam

*T*im & Lee Anne: *How much homebrew did you make at a time?*

Pam: Thirty-five gallons of homebrew, and after our farm commune broke up, my husband Woody couldn't keep up with that much beer. I was making big barrels for Woody, but there weren't enough people around to drink it. So it was getting like hard liquor towards the end. His gut was starting to hurt. One person can't go through that much beer, and I didn't cut the recipe down. We were throwing some out. In the winter, we would put it out in the greenhouse and let it freeze. And we'd drink the hard stuff on the bottom. God, I liked that! The water comes to the top and freezes and the alcohol stays on the bottom. It's really hard stuff. We'd be crawling across the floor.

How fast did you go through it?

In a week. We had thirty people in that commune.

Did you bottle it?

Somebody would bottle it every once in a while. But mostly we just dipped it out of the barrel. Some people wouldn't even wait for it to get done. Now I stick to Coca-Cola. I don't like homebrew. I don't drink. I drink a little wine every once in a while.

Tell about that time you gave it to the pigs. How come you gave it to the pigs?

Well, there was a disagreement among the commune. It was a bad evening just before Thanksgiving. '72? '73? I don't know, one of those years. So, there was this disagreement and everybody was pissed off. And we had this barrel of homebrew. I think it was 35 gallons. Dick was sitting in the chair talking to Charlotte and me about our problems and everything. We were all getting drunk. Feeling bad, really bad, right? And I get up and walk in the kitchen and Dick takes the glass and throws it right past Charlotte's head. It broke the plate glass window up front. I turned around and started cursing everybody out.

Was he throwing it at you?

No, he was throwing it at his wife. Charlotte was his wife. Oh man, I got so mad and went upstairs. Woody was in bed and I said, "Look, Dick just threw his glass through the plate glass window. I'm pissed off at this commune bullshit."

So Dick came up and apologized and everybody was ok. Woody says everything's fine. Well, I was still pissed. I went to bed, but I couldn't sleep all night. I was so pissed! So the next morning I got downstairs around four. It was getting light. Maybe five. And I went outside and saw all the snow on the ground. Enough to slide a barrel. And the pigs were just across the road. So I got the barrel and was dragging it out the front door and one of the other commune guys was just coming back from the outhouse. He helped me carry it down a couple of steps. I slid it down the front of the house and across the road where we had the pigs and poured it in the pigs' trough. This one pig comes up and oh my goodness! What's this? He comes and guzzles up the beer, then goes back and tells his buddies. We had six pigs at the time. Three of them died. We had to butcher them. Someone would go outside and say, the pigs are staggering around!

I finally said to everyone, "I fed 'em the homebrew."

Everybody said, "What! Fed the homebrew to the pigs!" Oh they were pissed. The guys kept going out dragging the pigs back into the huts so they wouldn't freeze to death. And the pigs kept staggering out and they'd drag them back. They were walking cross-legged! I never saw a drunken pig in my life. They were full grown pigs. They were ready to be butchered, but the meat tasted just like marinated pork. It was foul. I think homebrew will kill you.

Was that the end of it?
That was the end of beer. I said, no more. We'd buy some every once in a while. We had a bunch of meetings trying to get beer back into the commune, but I would say no. We were sober from then on.

Peter & Ina

I remember the first batch of homebrew we made was no good. We were living down on the river in Lewiston, Vermont, and we used river water. Connecticut River water and our friend Sidney's recipe and inspiration. I was at Dartmouth and he worked there. He was one of the very few people standing out under the flag for our weekly vigil about that war in '64. We got to know each other pretty well. Anyway, the river water spoiled it. Up here in the hills, the water is the thing. It's good.

We used hops right from the beginning. We sent for hops for the first three years, and then we moved here and there were hops! Right under the lilac tree. The only thing I've done is to kind of help them along as they go up the lilac bush, as they start to tentacle out looking for something to climb on. Next year I'll make some sort of arbor and sophisticate the production here.

It used to be hops and roses on the old farms. A cash crop. Every house had roses and hops. The two essentials. And usually some asparagus. It's funny. I was up with a friend a while back and we went into the field where he's going to build a new

Hops growing on the bine (Courtesy of Kris Anderson)

house. He'd been making a roadway. The tractor had churned up through the weeds and I looked and there was an old cellar foundation. I started looking around in the weeds, and sure enough there were some hop bines. With no place to grow. They were growing along the tops of the weeds and part of them were in the path that he'd run the tractor through a few times. But they were there. Right next to some asparagus and buried in the weeds. You could see where there was a little place about eight by thirty feet long in the side of the hill. Obviously that had been the old basic garden for the farmhouse. And hops and asparagus were right there. Whenever you find hops out in the woods it's always by a cellar hole.

Hops do well in the lilacs. They get up and go three or four feet above the top of the lilacs. The hop flowers hang down in the shade of the lilac leaves. They always have something to climb on, they look so healthy and lush. The hops on poles burn at the tips in hot summer weather. We'll harvest in another week, August 20th or so. It's hard to know because they go by so fast. They don't all come to the point of harvest at once.

Hops are harvested according to the general

herb harvest theory that you pick a day that promises to be super clear. You just know when you wake up that the dew is going to burn off. It's just after the dew burns off that you harvest herbs. Whatever the herb, wait until eleven o'clock or so when they're putting everything out to that flower. Harvest it then. Go up in the vines and pick the little flowers.

Prepare hops just like tea, steep but don't boil. In the beer wort three handfuls for ten gallons. It makes a wonderful sedative tea. And if you really want to sleep well, make a hop pillow.

Tom

I've been pretty faithful. I bet I haven't missed more than a couple weeks a year brewing in thirteen years. It's good for you! I don't get sick, and I tell people it's because I drink that good homebrew. The old bugs can't stand your body. People talk about health foods. I think homebrew is a real health food. It keeps your system organized. Daily bowel movements. Spring water has a lot to do with it. It would be interesting to go down and take some town water and make a batch, make it side by side. I bet there'd be a difference.

Here's another thing: You want to talk about food value? I've got friends who can't move in the morning without breakfast. I get up and I have about four cups of coffee and a glass of orange juice. That's all. I go about what I'm doing and about eleven o'clock, I have a quart of homebrew. I don't eat lunch until two o'clock or later and I feel fine. I've got energy and everything. There are some days when I don't have anything till supper. I don't drink enough to get drunk. I drink enough to give me some energy. I hate to say it, but I think that homebrew is just like a breakfast or a lunch.

My draft-style homebrew has got a lot of yeast in it. It certainly isn't clear. And yeast is a health food. In the last ten years, I've had maybe two colds. I make five gallons a week. I don't bottle in the winter because in the back room it works so slowly. It gets down real cold in there sometimes. I use bread yeast. Fleishman's. One package for five gallons. Seven cups of sugar. One can of malt. I use my caps again, because caps ain't cheap anymore. I use my caps maybe twenty-five times. Sometimes I bottle the whole batch, sometimes not. If I do bottle, I just rinse them out with warm water. I don't think it'll hurt you. You know everyone says clean the bottles, even boil them. But I don't ever get a bad bottle.

For siphoning off, I've got my hose resting on a block of wood so it just floats its way down in the crock and when it hits bottom it's not sucking all that yeast. And it goes a lot faster with this bigger hose. Sometimes when I've been just too lazy to bottle it, I've prolonged a batch a good whole week. I just put in some sugar every night. A pinch of sugar, less than half a cup. That way you can go three or four days without bottling.

I just did a batch a few hours ago, actually. Filled the garbage can up about half full with hot tap water, too hot yet for the yeast. I dump my malt in there because the good hot water will dissolve it. And dump my sugar in there. Then I add cold water till I like the feel of it. And meanwhile I've been dissolving my yeast in a cup of lukewarm water with a little sugar in it so the yeast is foaming. And then pour it in. That's all. It's very simple.

When I started making homebrew, Blue Ribbon malt syrup was under a dollar a can. In fact, when I moved here in 1965, the First National supermarket in Lebanon, NH, was getting 99 cents a can. (It's $2.35 now) I like the plain Blue Ribbon much better. The "pale dry" is too light. The plain malt makes a heavier beer, better beer. I find the other stuff tends to be more acidic or vinegary tasting. I don't like that. I only buy it in an emergency.

I'll tell you some of the other things I've tried. I've mashed up raisins and put them in a batch and it tasted a little different, but good. I made several batches chopping up apples and letting them float in the brew while it was brewing. Gave it a cidery taste. It was still homebrew but it had a little apple flavor. I've added pieces of orange and lemon. I've boiled some maple sap down. Maybe 30 gallons of sap boiled down to five and used instead of water. I don't think I added much sugar. I did put in malt.

I've also tried birch beer. Tapped yellow birch

trees and boiled that sap down. Some of that was horrible. But if you've got a bad brew there's still something you can do. A friend of mine built a little still. He used to run his bad brew through it, and he'd color it with burnt sugar—caramel—and you couldn't tell that from good whiskey! Very drinkable stuff. Take all the crud and distill it.

It's illegal, making whiskey or even beer. It's a federal law. Someone told me they were going to change it so it would be like wine. To make wine, you write down to the treasury department supposedly and get a permit to make 200 gallons or so for your immediate family's consumption. Technically you aren't allowed to serve your homemade wine to your friends. You can't even serve it to your cousins. I mean, it's ridiculous!

I've been questioned in the checkout line. I'll have six cans of malt syrup and a lot of yeast and sugar, and sometimes that's all I'm buying. They ask, what do you do with all this stuff? And I say, well, you can make good beer with it. They look real surprised. But there must be a lot of people making homebrew because they stock a lot of it. It says on the can that it's for fine cooking—"distinctive foods of agreeable flavor." I think it's a joke.

You ever heard of making champale? OK! After you're bottling and your yeast and all that junk is on the bottom, leave a few inches of dregs. Put in five gallons of water and your normal allotment of sugar. But no malt. And it's like champagne! It's real sparkly clear stuff. Made with just sugar and yeast. It fizzles almost like Alka-Seltzer and it tastes like a cheap champagne. You could make it stronger by adding more sugar. I use seven cups of sugar and sometimes ten. Champale is what we always called it.

I started brewing because of economics. Store-bought beer was getting out of sight. Now I generally prefer good bottled homebrew to tailor-made. It's better! It's certainly stronger, and it's cheaper. So maybe it's more than economics. There's another virtue of homebrew: I've been roaring drunk on this stuff and the next day I felt pretty good. That tailor-made beer with all the additives; I've had some fantastic headaches. I couldn't even walk the next day out to the garden. I felt so horrible. I've never felt that way with homebrew. It's pure.

I think Budweiser tastes horrible. You know why everybody drinks it? Because they see the ads and they see "the King of Beers" and they think that if they can't have a little piece of the action at least they can drink the most expensive beer. They may never drive a Cadillac, but they can have a Budweiser! The only time I buy any tailor-made beer is when I have friends come up for the weekends. They don't like the homebrew, and in some ways I don't want to share it with them either. Because they don't appreciate it.

John

No, I don't make it anymore. I just had too many drunks lying on the floor. In the morning you wake 'em up and give 'em coffee and they get up and start running around. And you know there's nothing worse than having a bunch of sober drunks running around.

INGREDIENTS: This Is About Beer; Questionables; Sue's Brew; The Flood of '76; Mountain Brewers, Orange County, Vermont.

Miller Pond Books • Strafford, Vermont

Back cover to the original edition (1975)

Stephen Morris (center), author of The Great Beer Trek, *enjoying some homebrew with friends* (Courtesy of Stephen Morris)

Afterword

AN EXCERPT FROM *THE GREAT BEER TREK* BY STEPHEN MORRIS

In 1978, Stephen Morris packed up a van with his wife and dog and set out across America to survey the country's much derided (at the time) beer culture. What he found was the beginning of a brewing revolution that would take hold decades later. Below is an excerpt from the book describing Morris's meeting with Tim Matson on his trip and his impressions of Mountain Brew.

My wife Laura and I are heading north into the Green Mountains and the hinterlands. Our destination is Strafford, Vermont, where we are scheduled to meet with Tim Matson, co-author of a simple tome on homebrewing called *Mountain Brew*.

The book, or more accurately, the booklet, was compiled and produced by Tim with no outside financing but lots of help from his friends. It was produced by a local woman's collective who knew as much about graphics as Tim did about home-brew. The cover was adapted from a drawing by a nine-year-old girl. Tim describes the experience: "It was a very pure thing. No deals, no contracts, no calculations involved . . . everyone just grooved along with the idea."

To describe *Mountain Brew* as a guide to home-brewing would be misleading. Rather, it is a description of a lifestyle for which homebrew is a spiritual center. From the craftsman's standpoint, the book is oversimplified. A hydrometer, the instrument used to measure unfermented sugars in the wort, is described as "made out of glass" with "numbers and lines on it." Some readers might object to a philosophy typified by statements like, "With food stamps I could make big batches of beer."

Its shortcomings should not keep one from enjoying the unique perspective of *Mountain Brew*. What the contributors lack in writing skill (in their defense it must be said that no pretensions of liter-ary proficiency were ever claimed), they made up for in ingenuity. Anyone discouraged by the blandness of American beers can look to *Mountain Brew* to learn about brewers who concoct experimental brews with Postum, wormwood, Maxim (to get a beer with caffeine), buckwheat groats, steak bones, chicken heads, maple syrup, and burdock root.

There are no mysteries about beer to the Green Mountain brewers. A simple product results from a simple process that the brewer controls. Some experiments result in improved beers, some in swill, but all will be consumed in a society that cannot afford waste. In Vermont, where winters are harsh and money is scarce, homebrew plays the role of balm, nutrient, and sacrament. This role would not be understood by the president of Miller or Schlitz. One of the contributors to *Mountain Brew* comments on beer's elevation to the status of a luxury beverage by saying this about Budweiser:

> *You know why everybody drinks Budweiser? Because they can see the ads and they see the "King of Beers" and they think that if that can't have a little piece of the action, at least they can drink the most expensive beer. They may never drive a Cadillac, but they can have a Budweiser!*

Somewhere an advertising executive reads this, pours a second martini, and gloats over a job well done. In Vermont, a flannel-shirted farmer sips on a second pint and feels the pain of a day of hard labor slipping away. Up there, they would say he is "blissed."

Tim Matson, author of *Mountain Brew*, is very much the mountain man on a smaller, more delicate scale. He wears the characteristic plaid wool shirt over a green jersey, blue jeans, and well-worn boots. He has dark, medium length hair with a few strands of gray, the sign of the transition period between unadulterated youth and middle age. He is polite, friendly, and unpretentious.

Tim offers tea, which we accept. His first batch of beer of the spring is just fermenting, so he had none to share. We sniff and taste the bubbling wort. It's going to be good. We talk about commercial beers. Tim's favorite is Narragansett Porter served on draft at the local roadhouse. He also likes Beck's and Busch, the latter not for its taste but for the claim of "no artificial anything." He is suspicious of any claims to purity made by commercial brewers. "*Mountain Brew* was a purity trip, because we all realized how overdosed all the food was. We were trying to get away from all that, to have some control over our lives, some order."

Tim's first experience with homebrewing was before he came to Vermont. He and some boarding school friends took cider, added raisins and Fleischmann's yeast, and stored the concoction in their closet. The inevitable explosion occurred on Sunday morning, just before church. Tim and his friends had no choice but to show up reeking of homebrew. He laughs at the memory. "I think my subconscious there had always been a feeling of rebellion associated with homebrew. Homebrewing is rebellion. It is for people who like to get high and people who like to have ceremony. Two pints and you're blissed. The gratification of making homebrew is much different than, say, pottery."

Tim tells us about his early days in Vermont, when homebrewing played as important a role in daily life as gardening or woodcutting. He and his lady brewed batches of fifteen gallons at a time. Friends were pressed into service, especially at bottle washing time. They wound up drinking more than they helped, but that was part of the process. Homebrew was used as a form of barter, as no one in the country had any money. It also ranked as the

#1 mountain folk house present. Working on the house, doing the garden, fixing the car; these were all passages of life accompanied by the ritual of beer. "Homebrewing is like making bread. It's not a matter of knowing how. Many people try it once, then never again. You have to be into the kneading of the dough. Homebrewing can be very boring. You have to be into your zen thing—hanging around the kitchen, washing bottles—it's work and you have to do it with the Spirit."

The tea is now gone, and Tim produces a six-pack of Beck's, that salty brew from the port town of Bremen, Germany, which we proceed to devour. The afternoon of the warmest day so far in the spring slips behind us. It becomes impossible to imagine how depressed we were on the morning of this very same day. The conversation turns philosophical, and then whimsical. The point to life, we somehow agree, is to drink good beer. Towards this end, Tim draws up a map to a local roadhouse and promises to meet us later on. There, he promises, this truth will be self-evident.

Acknowledgments

Mountain Brew was a collaborative project in its first incarnation, and so it is the second time around. This edition could not have happened without a group of fresh and seasoned recruits to lend a hand. Brewers and people connected to the beer world who helped include: Steve Polewacyk, Jeremy Hebert, Kris Anderson, the Addison Hop Farm, Alan Davis, Charlie Papazian, Kurt Staudter, Adam Krakowski, Stephen Morris, Betsy Parks, Joe Sherman, and Llama Lettow.

Adding archival material to the book was important to filling in the backstory, and for help with that thanks to Paul Carnahan and Marjorie Strong at the Vermont Historical Society, Bud

Haas, and Michael St. John. Special thanks to Blake Traendly for helping me reconnect with Heather Diana and Michael St. John.

I want to say a special thank you to the staff at the Countryman Press, today and over the past three decades, for their continuing support for a variety of my book projects. Special thanks my editor Dan Crissman, who responded with enthusiasm, book smarts, and beer savvy for this new edition.

I had the support and enthusiasm of kinfolk, especially my daughters Johanna and Mayellen, whose curiosity about homebrew helped inspire me to revisit the book. Jonathan Matson and Katinka Matson added valuable feedback during the book's journey.

The book would not have happened without the late Lee Anne Dorr, whose spirit lives on every page. It has been a pleasure to reconnect with her daughter, Heather Diana, who dug into the family archives for pictures to enhance the book. Her enthusiasm for the new edition added special energy to the project.

Vermont hombrewers celebrate the 50th anniversary of the repeal of Prohibition (UPI)